E. E Cothran

Smiles and Tears

In Verse and Prose

E. E Cothran

Smiles and Tears
In Verse and Prose

ISBN/EAN: 9783744652476

Printed in Europe, USA, Canada, Australia, Japan

Cover: Foto ©Thomas Meinert / pixelio.de

More available books at **www.hansebooks.com**

In Verse and Prose.

By E. E. COTHRAN.

SAN FRANCISCO:

THE SAN FRANCISCO NEWS COMPANY:

1882.

A ROMAN,
PRINTER.

PREFACE.

A preface is generally too hackney to contain anything very fine; yet it is a thing which every one expects to read in a new book, as much as an American audience expects its orator to begin with "Ladies and Gentlemen."

In spite of the affectations of the kid-gloved gentleman, whom to attempt to educate with good effect is as vain as plowing furrows in sand; in spite of the imbecile exclamations of the fashionable lady from her sofa—we still acknowledge that what now appears to the public in this little volume was mostly composed on a farm in the "vulgar country."

The author, laboring in common with all classes of men, necessarily added to his vocabulary of words a certain coarseness, which he fears must be only too clear to the really cultured and classical mind. Whether he should have kept silent, and drawn his cap over his eyes in the presence of such genuine illuminators as Bret Harte, Joaquin Miller, Hugh Bancroft, and Ida Coolbrith, or done as he has done, is not for him to declare.

The writer would repel the accusation that he has ever willfully assailed any true religious principle, though he would wish to be understood as desiring the destruction of superstition and hypocritical cant; for without religion, life is altogether a curse, and death is contemplated with un-

speakable terror. When we see our fellow-creatures, or when we our-
selves, lay away dear loved ones in the mute earth, to an unknown eternity,
we then most feel the sweetness and comfort of religious consolation; nor
would we exchange this feeling anywhere short of what appeared to us a
positive mathematical negation : much less for what is now but a sneering
doubt of its truth. Though the writer holds that all theological beliefs
have in them much absurdity and dross, he yet believes them to be a
manifestation of the human soul toward some ideal of purity and happi-
ness—a seeking after something higher and nobler ; and he further claims
that either mere skepticism or mere belief is no criterion of a moral or
an immoral life.

Inviting honest criticism, which he believes to be as applicable to the
advancement of thought as trimming to the outgrowth of trees, the
author briefly submits his labor for a respectful perusal : after which, if it
be thought a production of merit, let it be treated as such; but if proven
otherwise, let it be cast—as it should be—to the still sea of oblivion.

THE AUTHOR.

Smiles and Tears.

AN IDEAL.

To be with nobler minds and purer hearts,
  Than some beneath these skies ;
To live in worlds where the tear never starts
  In love's deep, tender eyes;
Where the forms and faces of those we love
  Their beauty aye retain,
Where the seraph of peace flies not above,
  Nor hope nor joy is vain.

CALIFORNIA IN NATURE.

Sun-kissed mountains of gold and snow,
Where sweetest airs 'neath heaven blow;
Of bright flowers, trees, and grasses green,
Where joy is heard and beauty's seen;

Shaded waters, glass-clear and cold,
That only birds and beasts behold;
Vales fair and useful as they smile,
Rich as the soil on Egypt's Nile;
Streams and rivers murmuring low—
Love's music when love's heart doth glow;
Near heaved the sea, solemn and deep,
And every ship was free to sweep;—
O'er all there ruled a savage race,
Of cruel soul and painted face,
Asleep in earth, their graves none know,
Hushed in oblivion long ago.

BABY'S SLEEPING ON HER LITTLE BED.

Baby's sleeping on her little bed,
   Her blue eyes closed in dreamless rest;
Soft around her move the angel dead,
   Companionship their subtle quest.

But she wists not of their mission,
   Though smiles of love and beauty wreathe her face;
She'll stay to be my moral Titian,
   Conducting me to holiness and grace.

MYSTERIES FOREVER UNKNOWABLE.

O, ever-changing brain of thought! thou art
At best the toy of fickle circumstance :—
O, heart! aching and bleeding with sorrow,
Or pulsing high with joy; strange the things which
Build or break thee.   Ah, mighty marble will,
How oft erecting fame o'er crime and death!
O, endless love! queen of philosophy,
So sad, debased by crowned ambition vile;
And fancy all absorbed, swift flying through
The airless climes of space.   What shall we know?
Shall we not seek for wisdom yet, but strive
To catch the secrets of eternity,
Though on our ears an awful bell doth ring
Mysteries forever unknowable?

TO A YOUNG FRIEND STUDYING FOR THE CATHOLIC PRIESTHOOD.

"It is not good that man should be alone,"
    So we read an ancient Man-maker spake ;
Another God now occupies his throne,
    Who would make men " eunuchs for the Lord's sake."

THE WORTH OF HUMAN LIFE.

Gold, power, place, or fame, can ye satisfy
    The deep, strong craving of a human heart?
Love sometime, but none now, thus breathe and die,
    And fail to live most men; better to dart
A carrion buzzard in the sunlight air,
    Change death to life from love of self and kind—
Ah, sweetest all when join some youthful pair
    In joy! heart linked to heart, and mind to mind;
Though flowers shall hide their hut, and poor their fare,
    And their dress be the peasants' plain attire,
Yet will they scorn foul wealth and tyrants dare—
    In life or death shall burn love's quenchless fire.

BURNS AND JEAN ARMOUR.

    " O, never fear, my Jeanie dear,
        I will na' leave thee in thy shame;
    So wipe away that bitter tear.

    My Jean, I love thee just the same,
        Howe'er the cruel world may sneer:
    Come to my hame—I'll take thy name."

" I would na' fear, my Robbie dear,
    If neighbor hearts like thine did beat;
But, oh! my sisters' scorn I hear.

And every brother gossips, too,
    Telling his friends, in careless tone,
How foolish fond I was of you.

I'll love and serve thee, Rob, for aye;
    If lost to you, what could I do,
But fawning harlot live—or die?"

"BOB BURNS."

"Bob Burns," the king of mirth and love and tears,
    Great tender soul, whose brains lay in his heart!
To millions' hopes and fears, for unknown years,
    His sweet Scotch hymns shall purer days impart.

THE PESSIMIST.

I.

I look above; the unfathomed sea of blue
    Heaves gently in the sun's eternal light;
The white clouds flee like ghosts before my view;
    Yet mystic beauty, majesty, and might

Are there forever : and the poor weak sight
  Of man sees little more ; for what may be
Beyond, he only hopes ; here day and night
  Make constant gaps in life ; and cruelty
  Alike with love, to us the Gods deal equally.

II.

Forever, worlds on worlds, the universe
  Of all, planless and purposeless, rolls on ;
That life to this, a blessing or a curse ;
  Chill darkness melts the golden rays of dawn ;
From all, nor First nor Last by us is drawn ;—
  Life, hope, joy, sin, sorrow, and death ; but then,
Mind at mystery eternal shall yawn,
  As hope made real would deify our den,
  And break the fencing round this universal pen.

III.

Ah ! where are those who sought to win the world,
  And those whose souls could never soar so high,
Yet whom around proud glory's banner furled?
  And where are they whose love all hearts should tie,
For whom charity now in vain doth sigh ;
  They who forgave their foes with dying breath,
Lived the kings of goodness, and thus did die?
  Wailing from the darkness, a Spirit saith :
  The gay, proud, poor, and great, as one are hushed in death!

THE OPTIMIST.

I.

To murder joy and be a coward pessimist,
   To be of darkling night and death and gloom,
Where self is all, yet naught—hail optimist!
   With thee is hope that sorrow cannot doom,
With thee love dies but once again to bloom;
   Though reason cannot sanction all desires,
She has in mortal hope an ample room
   To store up doubts; but naught can quench those fires,
Burning beyond nebular-light with love that ne'er expires.

II.

And minds supreme shall pierce the dark unknown,
   And love, sole joy to live, shall e'er entreat
The soul to hope, when all beside hath flown;
   The meek no more shall kneel at Sin's gay feet,
Weeping for justice; nor annals repeat
   Their old sad tale of youth and hope, in woe
And black oblivion to end; nor sweet
   Philanthropy remain loud pomp and show;
Nor power hide truth, nor peace breed ruin: for man shall know.

III.

Glorious guardians of the human heart
    Are songster, poet, orator, and sage ;
Forever, aye forever, they impart
    That heat which slowly burns the glacial age
Away; and like the ocean in her rage,
    With awful murmur bursting her confine,
Anon the right with wrong proud war shall rage ;
    And giant thought rude labor shall refine ;
    Catholic joy shall reign, birds sing, flowers bloom, stars shine.

TO ——.

Lady, why dost thou tell me
    Thou would'st marry for gold ?
Shame ! devils that now impel thee
    Have a strumpet's body sold !

TO MISS K——.

Tiny beauty, sweet unsuspecting maid,
    It were indeed a joy to view thy face;
Blue eyes with silken lashes overlaid,
    Grand brow which curls of gold so fairly grace,
        My wee beauty!

Pearl teeth that show and shine at love's bright jests,
    Sweet lips and pink-red cheeks—fond youth's delight;
I press thy royal waist and full, round breasts,
    Defying those that rant of wrong and right,
               Little beauty !

.

Naught pure as thou made blind old Homer see;
    Imogen, Juliet, are nice in play,
But none there are more natural, fair, and free,
    Than my sweet love, whose love words ne'er can weigh,
               Little beauty !

Things, time, and men may change, nor thou nor I;
    Love turn hate; hope, dust; truth and lies agree;—
But I'll know happiness if thou art nigh—
    In youth and age I'll live and love for thee,
               My wee beauty !

SHELLEY.

Shelley! imagination's spirit came
O'er thee; and thou didst pen in golden lines
The "fleeting beauty" of our mystic world—
And this for aye shall be the poet's fame;
Thou hast felt what many never feel,
Thou hast known what many never know,
And mad'st all viewless grandeur seem more real,
The source of truth or error, joy or woe.

TO A TURTLE-DOVE.

The fields were flaming red with fire,
  The pitiless wind would heed no prayer,
The grain was burned; the fiend would not expire,
  Though brave men sweat and struggled there.

When one, whose heart throbbed wild despair,
  Beheld a mournful dove, unheeding all
Save her charred nest and tiny unpiped pair,
  Which ne'er for love and food should call.

Sad tears came in the viewer's eyes,
  And then he madly rushed away;
Ye, who a creature's suffering despise,
  Picture this dumb bird's woe and mute dismay!

Poor dove! the cruel world glides on,
  Nor little cares for thee nor me;
The sun on fairer hope no more shall dawn,
  Now dark and dim in death and misery.

EXILED JEAN JAQUES ROSSEAU.

" Oh, for a home beneath the ocean waves,
    Or joyed to rest by the Siren's sweet song;
  To be with the mermaid as she laves
    Upon the billow's crest, or glides along

Bright coral gems, midst fairest mates that throng
  Her home, where the sad tone of music sounds
In primal purity and unknown wrong;
  Or to be I care not where, so the bounds
Are forever a limit to these man-shaped hounds.

"DESCENT OF MAN."

How theology's eyes did gape,
When Darwin said man was born of an ape!
'Twas begged of him some certain proof to show;
He answered: *Sirs! do not you ape for all you know?*

SOLOMON'S WAIL.

That face all loveliness to-day
Shall molder soon to common clay;
The loving heart and iron will
Erelong another place shall fill;
The mighty deeds of brain expanse
Shall come to naught through time and chance;
Trees, grass, and flowers may grow and bloom,
But rot they on their mother's womb;
Bright hymning orbs of boundless space
Sometime shall cease their joyous race;

All life of water, earth, and sky,
In one cold tomb shall silent lie;
What e'er hath been, or yet shall be,
Is vanity, is vanity!

LOVE.

While man is man, and sweet woman's woman;
    While ages lapse and Nature is the same,
And our souls are thrilled with passions human,
    Venus holier than Zeus we name;
Nor worlds of men nor aught can e'er defame
    One loving life, whose love doth make its might;
And as the stars with dazzling beauty flame,
    When darkness cold and blackly shrouds the night,
So angel love like them will be, and shine as bright.

TO A COMPLAINING MAIDEN.

Dear girl! the fairest flowers are often tilled
    Upon the most repulsive garden ground;
Strive to have thy soul with contentment filled,
    The best line life's wild-heaving sea to sound;
Strongest is the mind with hard duty drilled;
    Smiles win the love, for scowls no friendship's found.

THE DYING CHILD TO THE MATERIALISTIC MOTHER.

Dear mother, gaze into these dim, sad eyes,
Clasp these cold hands, feel if my heart still beat;
Am I myself, or something in disguise?
The tumbling world is moving far away—
How strange things seem, so fleeting, mystic all!
Now of black space I am the ghostly heir,
Through the chill darkness will my spirit race.
Shall I know where, or when, or what may be?
When I am gone, thou wilt behold of me
But food for crawling worms, or wreathing smoke,
Or ashes pale. Then, mother, canst thou think
That these alone survive mute mockery
Of thy sorrow? while I, whom thou hast loved
And hushed to peaceful sleep in babyhood,
With thy face a spirit-angel's shining,
Am blotted into nothingness—both heart
And mind forevermore! O, no! for thou
Wilt feel and know 'twere naught to live and love,
Though King-epherma in eternity;
If hope and joy and soul were only clay—
      To be and end like clay!

TO HER WHOM I LOVE.

To her whom I love,
I whisper above:
Happy be an angel,
Whom love can own;
Happy be an angel,
Whose life is for loan.

SOCIETY AND GOVERNMENT.

Society exists by common need —
Happiness is its universal end;
And government, as means should be decreed,
The evil to reform, the good defend.

YOSEMITE.

I.

Gaze down below, then turn thine eyes above,
If thou wouldst see a chasm in a dell,
Where Nature moves the heart to fear and love,
And all seems like a heaven,—earth and hell;
What stories may these mute creations tell

Of peerless beauty, majes'y, and might?
    Forever will remain their awful spell,
Dear to the memory as love and light,
Sublime as the rising sun or jewels of night.

II.

Here are beauties for Nature's worshiper;
    From huge uplifting forms of ancient rock;
From loftiest pine and towering fir,
    Whose roots around and with the former lock,
    And seem at all the heaven's storm to mock—
To the creeping moss and lowly flower,
    Which, like the humble man, should know no shock,
But have beneath the great a shady bower;
While they should breast the elements that have the power.

III.

Thou wilt fall forever, Yosemite!
    Man may his fellow-man subdue and chain,
Yet wilt thy waters leap both glad and free;
    While he doth live and die, thou wilt remain
    To teach mean tyrants freedom is not vain,
Nor ever poor slaves on the earth shall plod,
    Since perfect laws all liberty contain;
For who wholly owns air, water, and sod,
And who, by right, bows low before some base man-god?

IV.

Thy sweeping waters, with majestic tide,
  Fall sheer off and down the long and naked rock;
Yet still retain that which I love of pride,
  As on thy time-worn cliff they loudly knock,
  And sounding, surge like some electric shock.
My soul, which tingling nervously, doth glow
  With deep sublimity; as I yet lock
Mine eyes upon the falling water's flow,
Then gaze down to the white and foaming spray below.

V.

Bridal Veil, thy white waters represent
  The dress of now some fair and lovely bride;
And loudly then thy rocket forms present
  Signals fired of joy—but they swiftly glide
  Away and mingle with thy roaring tide.
And haste them to the dark and rolling sea,
  Where others soon will follow, and will hide,
Like those before, their own identity,
Till forth from the deep they come to eternity.

VI.

El Capitan, huge rock, silent and gray,
  The tall pines stand like pigmies by thy side!

Here once perhaps the red man knelt to pray,
　　Forgetting cruel deeds—the warrior's pride—
　　His scared voice lost in Merced's plunging tide ;—
O, look! bright rainbows dance round Bridal Veil
　　In thrilling grandeur, dazzling far and wide ;
On their beams, what radiant spirits sail ;
So beautiful! even dear woman's beauties pale.

VII.

I stand at midday on the Sentinel Dome :
　　Will life or death or aught efface this scene
And sight of Nature's own supernal home,
　　Of the wild peaks with wilder crags between,
　　Making with snow and sunlight golden sheen,
Lifting themselves like giants, huge and tall,
　　Above the gentle valley fair and green,
Where mists or thunders down the waterfall,
And near the soft blue sky of heaven spread o'er all.

VIII.

Starr King, thou art a heaven-reaching rock,
　　And look as though ambition fired thy clay ;
Ye almost touch the sky, and seem to lock
　　Yourself with clouds ; where, mighty throned, ye may
　　Mock all earthly tempests that beat their way

So wild and rugged; for ye lift your head
　　Where shines the sun in glory all the day;
Thy air no man can breathe, nor can he tread,
Where lone the bird of liberty his wings may spread.

IX.

South Dome, I see thy white and cloud-capt form
　　Reflected in the soft still lake below;
Upon whose mirror-face the sun shines warm,
　　Picturing vines and trees and rocks and snow,
　　With such sweet grandeur, dead to pain and woe,
That the soul fain would mix and melt away—
　　To be a part of earth, if it could go
And be of thee.—Alas! within our clay,
Pure love is oft a dream, and joys too soon decay.

X.

Ah! what is this dark and bright veering life?
　　We know no more than what we now have passed—
And that was mixed with hope and pain and strife,
　　Perchance with happiness, which soon was cast
　　Away, for discontent and sin did blast
And cower the soul—save of that chilling time,
　　When stifling moans and gasps shall be the last
Of earth; and then we hope in some bright clime
To know eternal love with mind and heart sublime.

XI.

The sun is slowly sinking from mine eye,
   And gloomily my heart his mellow light
Doth leave ; even in my infancy, I
   Felt the deep, sad impression, as the sight
   I saw in my mind till beautiful and bright
The spangled stars came peeping all around,
   And under heaven's arch, and soft and white,
The rolling moon danced lovely on the ground,
And as they banished sadness, gave a love profound,

XII.

That beauteous will be resumed once more :
   Ah, now ! I see the heavens all aglow
With warm and dazzling light, which, shining o'er
   And on the roaring waterfalls below,
   Makes what no soul with mortal words can know ;
E'en the eyesight seems some sweet delusion,
   And not the gleaming water and the snow—
Mantled mountains free from all confusion,
Though to the memory seeming an illusion.

XIII.

When to the massive cliffs and starry sky
   I look in silent awe, I marvel not

The poet's heart to such as these draws nigh,
　　Musing on all things unknown or all forgot ;
　　On what methinks must be a happy lot—
A lot as happy as a dream can be,
　　That has a universe with earth a spot,
And a deep immortal spirit, all free
To roam at will, in strong and soaring majesty.

XIV.

They of might and truth, like stars of heaven,
　　Shine forth when dreary is the world and dark,
And sink away when the daylight's given
　　Into their silent graves ; yet leave a mark
　　Of glory to mankind, who catch some spark
Of guiding majesty ; and they are stars
　　That light the sky, and burn above the bark
Of human dogs; in all life's pitiless jars,
Like Christ, they teach and pity those who cause their scars.

XV.

Now the setting moon throws her silver rays
　　In long, broad beams upon the hoary wall;
Then fades away; nor longer tranquil stays
　　A single star in heaven's spacious hall ;
　　But waning dim they slow retire, till all

The host have gone, and left me with my dreams;
　　But soon the twilight comes, and soon will call
The day; yes, now I see the craggy seams,
Where through and o'er the golden sun of glory streams.

XVI.

O, sweet Nature! I only wish to be
　　Thy constant lover: grant me but this boon;
Since I have seen thy work, Yosemite,
　　Can I forget and cease to love thee soon,
　　When spread around me are the sun, the moon,
The stars, the sky, and clouds, and winds that haste
　　To do thy will, and keeping one vast tune
With lakes, rivers, earth; and near by is placed
Round them "old ocean's gray and melancholy waste"?
　　JUNE, 1879.

INVOCATION.

Demons and angels of night and silence,
　　Now breathing dreams into the soul of sleep!
I'm standing 'neath the stars in sad suspense,
　　A mute longing in the everlasting deep:—
From the hushed mystery no spirit speaks;
　　The wailing birds whose lives are born of death,
The great gleaming orbs whirling swift around,

And the dull-chirping insects mock desire.
O, vanity and thought! I'll haste to bed,
　Where the spirit gropes for nothing higher
Than the strange dreaminess of peaceful rest.

HAPPINESS.

All men have spoken, all that bards have sung;
　With all that they can ever think or speak—
The life-worn brain often with but tongue,
　The wrongs heaped by the strong upon the weak;
The proud and sensitive heart which e'er shall seek
　A heaven's joy—but find of pain, a hell;
Tears shed, the soul that can nor weep nor break;
　The voice of fools, the thought in mind's deep cell,
　All, only the same strong hope for happiness tell.

JUSTICE.

Ah, Justice! twin-sister of Liberty,
　So hard to find: when found, so oft o'erthrown;
Thou showest how what is ought not to be,
　Thou stern, dim angel from the deep unknown!

27

The old, sweet dream of Justice, fair and pure,
Ever wakes to sad decrees in Nature ;
Fools, kings, wars, riches, rascals still endure,
And slavery binds the human creature.

WOMAN'S LOVE.

Life's vain without some woman's love—
Pure love that spirits hymn above ;
Without which, all would fiendish be,
Whether beast, man, or Deity.

TO BABY.

Angel babe, none have hate nor fear of thee,
   Who know the beauty of thy tender heart ;
See thine eyes swimming tears or dancing glee,
   Hear thy tones more than a sage's word impart.

Health's rose-red cheeks, high brow, both broad and fair,
   Eyes as sky or far-distant mountain blue ;
Thou sweetest child and babe of silken hair,
   In thee I look the highest heaven through.

In my arms, thy heart beating close to mine,
   Little lips giving Nature's purest kiss;
I know the world's hypocrisy is never thine—
   That love and life for thee bring holiest bliss.

And should'st thou grow as cruel, base, and vile,
   As thou art innocent and stainless now,
I would love thee; though on me curses pile—
   Such hath been who will learn both why and how?

For, oh! upon this airy sea of life,
   How oft our joys are ruined, and hopes are fooled;
How oft 'tis shrew and man, and brute and wife;
   Failure in youth and prime, dark death when schooled.

PUBLIC CUSTOM.

The laws and "powers that be" are sometimes wrong,
   Slaves of custom to countless lies conform;
As public thought, no tyrant is so strong,
   Nor leaves so few the many to reform.

SUCCESS.

We believe and live in our desires,
　　We toil and hope for what we love,
Unthinking where the truth may be ;
　　And fear of power and mystery
Is deemed the mean for every end—
　　The one real end is happiness.
What servile praises follow him,
　　Who, by his natural strength, or by
Some smile of circumstance, shall win,
　　Fame or money!　Be this success,
How many can on earth succeed?
　　And noble love, and friendship dear,
And pure joy in the spirit's realm,
　　The holiest and sweetest things in life
Shall be forever to mankind
　　As the red-hearted lily, grown
From dank and filthy scum; to be
　　Plucked by pleasure-drawn youth, and left
To die in its silent beauty;
　　Or as ocean-bubbles, the wave
Of might shall strike and bear away.

" SWEET LAND OF LIBERTY."

No country's free where self is king;
    Real liberty does no deeds inhuman,
But grants the natural rights to everything—
    The rights of every child, man, and woman.

Boast not America is fair and free,
    While far from self-ruled is her government,
While robbed are innocence and honesty,
    By dark intrigue and courtier blandishment.

WHY!

Canst thou bind the sweet influences of the Pleiades, or loose the bands of Orion?—
Job xxxviii : 31.

List to the music of the starry choir,
View, wonder-struck, those whirling balls of fire;
Travel the sea, behold her gentle sleep,
Or hear the thunder of her awful sweep;
Scan old earth's geology, each page,
From first of seven to the present age;
Pierce, if thou canst, that far-off sphere of gold,
Through the heaven of blue sublimely rolled;

Deep study with philosophers the soul,
Or superstition with thy thoughts enroll;
Stand silent o'er the tomb, and hot tears weep
For dearly loved one hushed in peaceful sleep;
Let love, planting flowerets on the grave,
Ere long so bright and beautiful to wave
Her way through dim and mystic darkness wend,
Hoping still howsoe'er each hope shall end.
In the forests of America roam,
Where million reptiles, birds, and beasts have home;
On the wide river of Amazon row,   .
And all her nested fowl and fishes know;
Or proud explore the pole of icy breath,
Where waking or sleeping, life most is death;
Live in hazy mirage of scorching flame,
Idly lewd and strange to the blush of shame;
Columbia, Asia, and Europe praise,
Where 'tis claimed religion or reason sways;
Minute atom of an oblivial hour,
Why rob thy brother of his power
To think and love, and make him toil and bleed,
So counting glorious thine evil deed?
Man, seeing, doing thus, wilt thou pretend
To know why all exists, and why shall end
In separation of the universe,
In harmony with that ye love or curse?

ON MISS ——.

Oh, she was a beauty!
 So loving, sweet, and pure;
To kiss her was love's dear duty;
 Though kisses, love will never cure.

Smoother than Angelo's marble,
 Her sacred intellectual brow;
And her voice like birds that warble
 Sunshine and joy—you know not how.

And then to look upon that eye,
 And read the very spirit there;
Her love and hope and goodness high,
 Free, spite the deeds of Aidenn's pair.

Ideal form of angel grace,
 Infinite sweetness in her smile,
Strong beauty of a woman's face,
 A power that can the heart beguile.

O, she was a bonnie beauty!
 So loving, sweet, and pure;
To kiss her was love's dear duty;
 Though kisses, love will never cure.

DANIEL WEBSTER.

O, Webster! thou wert king of mind and heart,
    The chief of statesmen, dead or living now.
Up from thy chair, I see thee listless start;
    But soon thine eyeballs flash beneath thy brow,
    And all before thy mighty words must bow;
Nor time nor eternity ne'er can rive
    Them from the spirit's memory; and thou,
Who did with majesty and beauty give
Such thoughts to man, may'st say forever—"I still live."

HOME.

With strong sire and gentle tender mother,
    With toddling babe and loving wife, to live;
With the pure sister and noble brother—
    What sweeter hope or joy this life can give?

Home! O, sweetest blessing or blackest curse!
    Dear as our hope of everlasting joy,
Or sad as the atheist's universe,
    Heaven of life or hell that will destroy.

2

HERMIT OR HUSBAND.

Often removed from man, we contemplate
  His as a sad and selfish lot—
A creature of instinctive fear or hate ;
  Most hopeless and most sinful blot
Upon the page of Nature's lengthy book.
  Thus may we grow the Harold of unrest,
So earth can give no loving nook
  Where gently heals the torn and bleeding breast;
And scowling fierce from bitterness of soul,
  Misery or madness blacken each day;
The fiery heart heeds not control,
  Till to quiet darkness it burn away :
Not so with him who lives and toils with man,
  And with some maiden views the stars,
While joyous children laugh within the van,
  Proud dancing on the throat of Mars;
He, like a perfect flower, shall only fade
  When full of fragrance is its time;
He, like the sonnets cherubim have made,
  Moves on in everlasting rhyme.

TO A LADY FRIEND.

Ah, dear lady! though thy words were sincere,
 Which bade me cross the threshold once again,
I come no more; the place would be a sneer
 To all my youthful dreams and hopes—and then
'Twere best for me to hide deep in my heart,
 What might have been, but now can never be.
Farewell to her!—I bear the cruel dart,
 To pain this side of dim eternity;
Farewell to love of speechless joy and pride,
 So pure and holy in the vanished days:
I thought all passion in its time had died;
 But no; mine lingers and forever stays!

WOMEN'S RIGHTS.

Fair and lovely sister, faithful woman,
 In your virtue throned a sacred beauty;
Your love in law must still uplift the man,
 As goodness is thine, whate'er thy duty.

Man takes your money to help force his law,
 As kings took his a hundred years ago;
Why stand—as stood your brother then—in awe,
 Thousands afraid to strike for truth a blow?

Alas! that right should fail for want of might,
    And noble souls o'er cruel acts repine;
And patient love be voiceless in the night,
    While brutes and thieves, in part, her place define.

If by the people, governments are made,
    Man can only equal be to woman;
And why should power's conceit be but obeyed,
    If justice and law be fair and human?

THOUGHTS OF THE PANTHEIST.

From the low grave—sad and silent dust—
Where alone life meets the dim forever,
Countless thoughts and hopes; and alas! base fear
Come wailing to the human soul for light;
Such things must be; for of all life and death
Each mind will have its own philosophy,
And that which forces vows of public belief,
Bears cringing slaves and shrewd hypocrisy.
Know thou the tear-wet tomb? hope knows no tomb,
Nor eternal love, nor tranquil reason;
They sing at parting this grand requiem:
Matter to matter, and force to force, and mind
To mind; all things do merely change, and all
There is has ever been, and e'er shall be;
All limits each, and each thing limits all,

From crowned intellection to the viewless
Atoms; and they, who leave effect to dream
Of one first cause—author of all we hate
Or love, of woe or joy, of wild despair
Or sweetest hopes—become but worshipers
Of power, making chaos of pure ethics.
Some mind must be supreme; yet only all
The unmade everlasting universe
Of matter, mind, and force is infinite:—
When superstition shall no longer be,
And man shall strive to reverence principle ;
Give public praise to pure morality
Unmixed with fable of the vast unknown,
Give conscious sin a general curse
With justice to creative circumstance,
And real religion dawns upon the world.
'Twill yet be—though thought still is weak—and hope
Before the base idols of past ages,
Weeping, died to sad memories of dreams.
Time and thought so change, that the ideal
To-day, to-morrow hath a funeral,
Sepulchered ever with our passing tears,
Or transient scorn, or mortal fancy eyes
The whole as cycles of eternity.
Like man, nations have fallen into rack
With wild experiment, with luxury,
Negligence and crime, and none has ever
Blossomed to its own desire of truth
And beauty; yet hope (that palmer—angel
Whose travels reach beyond the stars) still holds

Sweet jack-o'-lanterns to the eyes of man.
In our tearful speechless sadness, we gaze
Upon the dimmed and vacant eyes of death,
And the charity, which in life, had made
A seraph of a fiend, we give in vain :—
Hateful to the soul of sense and goodness,
Those solemn radicals who hear and judge
For aye, by their small village law, the poor
Pleas of sin and sorrow—cease thy judgment;
For the Spirit is a complex problem,
Scorning pure reason, and the richest lore,
Even herself; her native self to know.
O, whirl, forever whirl, bright shining worlds!
Creatures of light and darkness, we will laugh
And weep, love and hate, hope and fear, as now,
Till we submit to your unchanging rules,
Not with sad and hopeless yearnings; but with
Healthy reasoning and gentle patience,
Grasping joy in the holy days of peace.

BEETHOVEN, MOZART, AND MUSIC.

I.

Songs sad with sin, or sweet with purity;
   Beethoven and Mozart made the whole earth
Holier voicing hidden melody;
   Eternal heirs of glory from their birth,
   Sublime beings that are of far more worth

Than those whose heads with golden crowns are set—
 Than those who rule the world with blood and dearth,
And whom we e'er should hate—if not forget,
Beside these names to which the world's praise is a debt.

II.

I saw Beethoven touch nis instrument;
 Thrills of deep feeling through his frame would tear,
His face was full of joy and heaven-bent,
 Communing with the spirits of the air.
 Above, around, beneath, and here and there,
Was heard the awful sound of moving worlds;
 Happiness was sung; pain that women bear;
Men's hates and fears; the laugh of boys and girls—
And all, through life and death, in passive grandeur whirls.

III.

A universe of darkness round the soul,
 Where monsters yell in rage and fear and pain;
Now huge red waves through hell in chaos roll,
 And then the sun, like lightning's flash, again
 Bursts forth; no clouds, nor even mist remain
To hide the bright blue sky; beautifully
 Earth's sounds and sights all blend within the strain:
O, airy angels, love and melody,
And thou, sweet music, Heaven or death are in ye!

HUMAN RIGHTS.

" Your rights can only cease where mine begin,"
 There for aye uphold your independence ;
The " might makes right " has been our hellish sin,
 Not one fair form with snakes' attendance.

POLICY.

Some passions in this man are strong and deep,
 And reason may be fettered weak or low;
If thou wouldst have his love, and it wouldst keep,
 Now to his nature suit thy words, then slow
 To thine own thought return—and as storms blow
Gentle currents alike with them at will,
 As little streams to winding rivers flow,
So, drawing him to thee, thou must fulfill
What else had failed, devoid of policy's nice skill.

HENRY CLAY SPEAKING AGAINST THE ADMISSION OF CALIFORNIA AS A SLAVE STATE.

There he stood all alone,
   Like some dying soul in isolation;
Proud his aspect, prouder his tone,
   As gazing upward with a tearful eye,
He besought the justice of another realm,
   If justice here below should die;
Those thin blue hands were clasped in awful scorn
   Of the base mummies grouped around;
For they but images of men were born,
   Beside that soul so lofty and profound!

CHARITY'S DIVINE.

To dry one burning tear,
   To heal one bleeding heart,
To calm one deathly fear,
   Is doing no small part.

To guide one soul aright,
   On life's sad face to smile
With love's beauteous light,
   Is surely worth the while.

Human and tender be,
  Whatever faults are thine;
Sweet is fair purity,
  But charity's divine.

THE PEACE OF LIBERTY.

Amidst the ills of life,
In gloom and doubt and strife;
    Where hopes and fears
    And jeers and sneers;
Where woes and joys and pains—
Comprise all earth contains.

I've sworn within my mind
Some sweeter peace to find;
    If from outside,
    None shall divide
True love and hope with me,
I still breathe proud and free.

In peace with all to be,
Save when base wrongs I see;
    Free heart and brain
    I will retain
While being's tide shall flow,
And I its course can know.

THE MUSE'S THRONE.

Away in the firmament's azure blue,
    Where beams the mighty soul of day so bright;
Beneath the moon and stars, where love may woo
    And win in the still loveliness of light,
    Among her worlds of pure unfathomed light;
Where the ocean rolls in an eternal moan,
    And the high mountains ever loom snow-white;
In forests where the birds have sung and flown,
    And aye the great and tranquil rivers run;
    Where flowers and herbage spring beneath the sun,
And nor air nor earth whispers human groan,
Are set the poet's heaven and the muse's throne.

SELFISHNESS.

Shall selfishness be ever king of man,
    When man of selfishness should be the king?
Must happiness forever be a ban,
    Because the soul is thought by some a thing
    That may be bought and sold for what 't will bring?
Oh! must we toil and seek earth's gold to find,
    To look like Zeno down on suffering?
Or shall we wish the power of Shakspere's mind,
Unless it be to love and benefit mankind?

Dost thou not care if one poor heart be sad ;
  If million burning eyes are closed in tears ;
If hope and love are gone, and mind be mad
  With sin and men—and no more darkly fears ;
  To sleep and test that hope which so endears
Itself to man ? Is all as it should be
  When human hearts may throb through all the years
Of time ? What is the grand humanity,
All joyless here for an unknown eternity ?

LIBERTY, EQUALITY, AND FRATERNITY.

There are more liberty, equality, and fraternity in a pioneer
than in a long-settled country—and why ?

Because man's environment in a country new to civilization
favors such a state of things ; because, also, where the savagery
of nature is to be changed and conquered, the reckless brave, the
lovers of wild adventure, and the spirits of proud honor go.

There, amid hardships, chance injuries, and terrors innumer-
able, the persecuted part of humanity has gone, forever, in search
of more perfect freedom : but, alas! their cradles have rocked
but few generations of patriots and heroes.

Before proceeding further, we would make the broad state-
ment, with the vast tomes of historical experience at least partially
in view, that a limited number of individuals control and direct
all, or nearly all, the political systems, religious beliefs, and financial
movements of the world ; and when these prevent each other from

tyranny and oppression, by being somewhat equally balanced in power and influence, there is left considerable liberty to those who have the courage to select independent positions.

This end was at one time almost reached in the United States; but now, though there is tolerable freedom in religion, the people are fast being chained by the evil leaders of politics and finance; and such is the situation, that, to succeed in the war for office and wealth, one should become an arch hypocrite, and often a thief; and so seldom can the duped people provide just punishment, that success—no matter how obtained—has come to be worshiped as the great "I am" of existence, a thing which means merely the acquirement of gold, and which covers more sins than does charity.

That these social dangers are an effect of fierce competition that results from an increasing population, and the heterogeneity of the people, as much as of criminality and ignorance, cannot be doubted.

Having noticed individual control, and an example of it in the United States, it is fit to learn how, and how far, the opposite state has been developed.

First, in a newly settled country, particularly where the inhabitants are cosmopolitan, politics, finance, and religious opinion are without method, unity, or powerfully established leadership; and when men are thrown confusedly together, to view each other's clashing customs, beliefs, authorities, and absurdities, feelings of diffidence, of honor, and the common sense born of a little observation, forbid any one of them boldly asserting his superiority, or right of government, over the rest of them; yet, even here, where the greatest equality and truest brotherhood are realized, men do, from necessity, search out and gladly accept an informal leadership of their best talents.

For a while their progress is peaceful and swift; but soon the prudent scheming few build up capital upon the simple carelessness of many, and slowly and naturally grow stronger and more ambitious of power, until the final effect—as the history of nations proves—is a consolidation of tyrannical aristocrats, with a mass of slavish, ignorant humanity beneath them. Most countries of earth furnish to-day a clear example of this last-mentioned phase of government; and especially do the Chinese, Russian, and British autocracies.

When we think of the United States without patriotic prejudice; when we contemplate, however hopefully we can, the fearful effects and influences of their corporate monopolists; the increase of worthless population; the frequency and enormous cost of elections; the multitudinous number of officials; the great and myriad interests, spread over vast territory, necessarily conflicting with each other; and, worst of all, the buying of votes, and defiance of just legal restrictions, by political rulers and powers, we are forced to believe that a pernicious society, and a most corrupt and dangerous government, are being rapidly created.

Must we, then, go on in the future as we have gone in the past, ever seeking, but never finding, a remedy for all this trouble of powerful and gluttonous aspiration, of imbecile and religious starvation?

Very little practical truth, but much ideality and absurdity, has been evolved from this question.

Among the most baseless opinions that have considerable circulation just now, is one which holds that capital creates labor and wages, and is the direct cause of their rates, instead of the amount of labor to be done, and the number and skill of those who are to do that labor. We do not deny that capital is a necessary aid to difficult and complex labor; but we do claim that nothing—not even capital—could be produced without labor. While considering it the duty of honest people to ever and everywhere prosecute rich rascals and their knavish supporters, we are far from siding with that senseless, uproarious class which is always passing political resolutions that are drawn and drafted by demagogues, who, for incompetency and idleness, have been forced from the fields of legitimate labor.

Another intended relief is found in "the doctrine of holding all things in common"; which, though we are compelled to pronounce beautiful in the sight of abstract justice, is, in the present state of civilization, wholly impracticable; for its most successful votaries—Mother Ann's little flock—in their attempt at its practice, are said to have destroyed the supreme happiness of life, familiary affection, and comfort in relation to posterity. For any known form of government to have an exclusive possession of all real estate, thereby aiming for an equitable division of "perishable property," which, *apropos*, contains all needful values to existence apart from those which are natural, might, with purer motives and higher reasoning, be successful; but a general attempt to practice this theory now would, we think, only stay individual effort and energy: for what Vanderbilt would permit a million beggars to extract coin at their pleasure from his pockets? That beggars, in preference to toiling like honest men, would thus satisfy their wants, did any method of the distribution of the result of labor allow them, is a little too plain. And finally, as great difficulties as those disturbing the system now in vogue close around the aforementioned theory of the correct controlment and true ownership of property, namely: production, taxation, and distribution which will be just, equal, and uniform, and which a government of either force or liberty can rightly arrange and enforce.

Shall we then have recourse to the old bloody revolutions, whose clouds have scarcely rolled from the sky till they begin to blacken it again? Shall we have union and co-operation of labor in all its departments, though for which trained intelligence is required; and also the moral stamina to resist the flattering allurements of a powerful opposition?

Either not discerning or believing the foregoing devises to be inadequate, the American revolutionists thought they saw a final and complete remedy in general education for this sad tendency of governments; and early in the history of our country, the institution of free public schools received loud and prolonged agitation. Still it was overlooked by many, that the construction of human nature opposes the practicability and permanency of the desired result of the plan; for it is absolutely certain that the ratio of intelligence to ignorance must ever on earth remain the same. That no amount of education can make a genius of a fool, is much too evident.

An intense individuality has predominated in all ethical, political, and financial systems that have had an influence over the world. Public opinion to-day once rested silently in the original brains of a limited few; and we may in truthfulness still further assert, that inidviduality is the efficient cause of all human advancement or disturbance; for in individuality we find the beginning of every original thought and deed. To scientists, philosophers, warriors, statesmen, poets, orators, musicians, and artists, are the masses of mankind subordinate, and indebted for progress or retrogression.

Since these leaders of the social structure are immeasurably the product of circumstances, often immoral, and liable to comparative ignorance—thus being likely to lend their whole power and precedent to the establishment of evil principles—the sorrowful question confronts again, Will mixed evil and good forever be the portion of the populace? Without further argumentation, we would answer, No!—more, we admit, in hope than in knowledge.

But, withal, is it irrational to think, that, when scientific attainments have become—as they surely will—greater and grander, material environment will favor a higher and nobler state of being? that, with more perfect physical conditions, the now fanciful millennium of philosophical and ethical beauty will be a sublime reality? To them who have hope, and to them who have no hope, of some such end, we may, in the mean time, propose alike for their following the highest ideal of earthly conduct: Do what good you can, both for yourself and humanity.

ODD SAYINGS.

Every man loves what to him seems good; and what to one seems good, to another seems evil.

All are alike in search of happiness, though many never learn the way thereto.

Mystery of mysteries! Nature encircles all life and death, nor shows her beginning nor end.

Better no birth than a birth to misery.

That which shows itself to the senses should be believed and followed, rather than that which does not.

3

Be not submissive to tyrants like Cæsar, for their thrones are built on the misery of man.

Women and men should be equally free in all the workings of life, so nothing may be one-sided.

Alas! what ought not to be, is ; and what ought to be, is not.

Greatness that is meek, like some resplendent jewel which seeks not, but is sought, is the center of desire.

Love greets love with outstretched arms; but fear flees to hide, still finding no rest.

They are damned whom no one loves.

Man's law seeks to preserve more than reform; but love's law, through eternity, seeks conversion.

As birth and teaching may form the mind of man, will he do that which is good or evil.

Might and right united are like a sun before which every star of night shall grow dim.

The moral liver is known only by deeds, and never by confession or profession; as a smart rascal may be a devil in reality, and an angel in pretension.

An error of honesty is better than the perfection of hypocrisy. Sorrow is transient: swift run the hours of night; soon comes the day-star's golden beauty.

Deep in the heart of an old ugly mountain rich treasures are often hid; while brass and mica gleam everywhere.

If all necessarily be for the best here, all must necessarily be for the best hereafter. The fool should receive our mingled pity and scorn.

They who have power, and are foul therewith, will be loved only by worms in the end.

IMMORTALITY—AN ESSAY.

Is the word immortality the symbol of a sublime fact, or of mere meaningless imagination?

We must answer this query with either theory or science. However dark the mysteries which close around us, we cannot be silent upon this question, while the aching brains of sages, the mute sorrows of broken hearts, the eyes wet and dim with burning tears, and the holy, peaceful kiss that everlasting love imprints upon the cold and speechless lips of death—all ask if mind, with its sad and sweet humanity, shall have in some form or place a conscious hereafter, or forever sleep inane!

Indisputably, one or the other of these conditions must be the finality of all earthly intelligence.

Probably no one lives who could adduce many original truths toward this discussion ; for individual thought—though sovereign from a human standpoint—is like a frail ship that sails upon a shoreless ocean, which is the universe, and leaves behind tiny eddies, ephemeral as lightning. Yet the ocean and ship exist : should reason or fancy hold the helm? Let us decide that as we sincerely can, but ever be charitable to those who are against us.

Desiring to be somewhat methodical, we have embodied our deductions of this subject in the order of numbered propositions, upon which, when given, the negative and affirmative evidence may be weighed.

PROP. 1. A change called death must, according to some law or laws, affect all material organizations ; but that any can be brought to nothingness, is inconceivable.

Prop. 2. That any kind of organization of matter can be effected without either force or mind, is also inconceivable.

Prop. 3. The universal germ must be an inherent and eternal existence.

Prop. 4. That the first principle is matter alone, force alone, or mind alone, is unthinkable, and opposed to all knowledge, whether empiric or innate.

Prop. 5. That the germ is only matter and force, is beyond credence; for when these are analyzed and synthetized in all their myriad varieties and changes which are under the eye of science, they nowhere seem capable of producing mind.

Prop. 6. That the universal germ is mind, matter, and force—self-existent, yet dependent one upon another—is in closest agreement with demonstrated facts.

Prop. 7. The human mind must comprehend the first principle as entirely unlimited; and as all known or conceivable mind, matter, and force *are each in themselves limited*, no one of them can account for the being of the other two, so naturally we compose the first principle of them all together.

Prop. 8. Thought, sensation, and life are to themselves invisible, and generally—perhaps always—reciprocate through the medium of matter; nor can there be a mental communication *altogether* free from material objectiveness, which, though, might be of countless characters, shapes, or distances.

Prop. 9. Matter of itself does not move; but matter with convertible force does move.

Prop. 10. Without matter there could be no force, for there would be nothing for force to act upon.

Prop. 11. There could be no mind without matter or force, for every thought or fancy always is in a measure objective; nor can there be absolute if any subjectivism, no more than the idea of a horizontal line void of its perpendicular.

Before the condemnation of dogmatist shall be made, will the reader carefully and candidly examine the given propositions? The writer will then be prepared to specify more particularly on this speculative subject. Is mind eternal? Some have said: "If I am eternal in mind, why do I remember no other objective reality than of this sphere; why is my mind unconscious of existence prior to that it now has"? It may be answered, that we do not remember all objectiveness here, even, except by suggestion or association.

That the composition and character of the objective state of another world is, perchance, much different from ours, and would therefore awaken different memories; and that mind, upon the death of its personal possessor, may undergo an incomprehensible mutation. (See Props. 8 and 11.)

Many of those who are skeptical of the eternal existence of mind have stood upon an equal hight with the most acute and gigantic thinkers of the world, and present to our consideration a vast array of sophistical and axiomatic evidence. These intellectual materialists claim that man, being an animal himself, is, in his relation to the hereafter, at par with all flora and fauna which derive their substance and vitality from earth and sun. None will deny that this is true, so far as physical properties and life forces extend; but if the proposition shall any further retain its value, it must, at least, be made probable that mind, like structural life and vegetation, is the mere conditional attribute of matter and force.

An organization of life devoid of mind or of instinct, or of both, might, by some abstruse possibility, be produced from matter by electricity, magnetism, heat, etc.—as electricity alone is capable of converting force into motion ; and motion, wherever it be, is almost identical with the life in an organization. But where, in water, earth, air, and space, is there a thing which could create mind but mind? (See Props. 5 and 6.)

Yet, it is said that as mind is dependent upon matter and force for its every manifestation, it is therefore resultant from them. Now, a plant proceeds from matter and force, which, when analyzed in the plant, are found to be of *exact quantity and quality*—even to coloring agents and substance—that they were originally, and will be when the plant has undergone disintegration. Then the plant, by its chemic construction, proves itself an identical origin from matter and force; but these, nowhere under our observation or sensation, even in electric phenomena, evince any distinct sameness to mind. (See Props. 5 and 7.)

Diverting slightly, we may say it is certain that matter is dependent upon force, and inversely; yet none holds the one as an attribute or effect of the other, nor denies their eternity. (See Props. 9, 10, and 6.)

Nevertheless, it is further urged that instinct is something between which and mind no plain line can be drawn, and that the former still reaches such an extreme blindness as to be almost inseparable from natural physical forces.

We confess this is a most powerful objection to those who simply believe in the immortality of the human mind; and for this kind of argument, we, who take another position, have no defense. (See Props. 1, 2, 3, and 6.) And neither can we pretend to know whether instinct is a blind force, or a lower order of mind; but in the face of our observation and experience, the latter appears to be the likeliest conclusion. (See Props. 4, 5, and 6.)

Let us grant, for the sake of a brief reflection, that we are not immortal, and all mind shall at last cease to be; what would it matter? Nothing; for there is no desirable condition of mind, except that condition have its complement in mind. Imagine only one mind in the universe; how wholly useless and vain its existence would be if it were similarly constituted to ours: however, imagine two or a million minds; how full of meaning to each other and one another—though to nothing else—their existences become.

The independence and eternity of mind, matter, and force being granted, we must of necessity be immortal; but exactly how or where our intelligence is continued, is a problem beyond the solution of the mightiest reasoner. (See Props. 7 and 8.)

The ignorant, in the future as in the past, are likely to transform, in imagination, their earthly ideals to the "shining shore," and their hatreds to the "bottomless pit"; for as long as there are mysteries there will be ignorance; though it is to be hoped there will yet be more wisdom. Were there no evidence toward, and nothing save, the bare hope of immortality, we, on account of temperament, would likely indulge in such hope. The extent of the aforenamed belief may be approximated by the vast number of prevalent theologies, which, in their "divinely inspired revelations," authorize the hope of a continuance of existence in another realm.

We do not, withal, contend that these hopes and beliefs, (our own included) form any reasonable basis for an argument supporting ideas of immortality; but have, we think, through the sanction of tradition, custom, and public opinion, become, as it were, "a part and parcel" of our natures, wherein they remain sensitively strong and enduring. And of these, whatever is false will slowly perish, violently or peacefully, as adverse to scientific truth and investigation. Though the jewel case be broken for its unfitness, the genuineness of the jewel—if it be jewel—will in nowise be impaired.

Nothing is too humble, nothing is too august and high—from the dim and distant nebulæ to the microscopic insect—that we, for *fear of public odium*, should refrain from its examination ; but only the consciousness of inability, and hence the uselessness of exploration, should compel us to desist.

Professing to be without prejudice in reviewing what evidence we are capable of discerning, we are wholly satisfied to rest our hope and knowledge upon the side of immortality.

www.ingramcontent.com/pod-product-compliance
Lightning Source LLC
Chambersburg PA
CBHW030719110426

42739CB00030B/1000